GRANDPARENTING: Continuing the Journey with GENERATION Z

CONTINUOUS *Engagement and Sharing*

with

CONTINUAL *Support*

Mary Ellen Davis

Gotham Books

30 N Gould St.
Ste. 20820, Sheridan, WY 82801
https://gothambooksinc.com/

Phone: 1 (307) 464-7800

© 2023 *Mary Ellen Davis*. All rights reserved.

No part of this book may be reproduced, stored in a retrieval system, or transmitted by any means without the written permission of the author.

Published by Gotham Books (November 28, 2023)

 ISBN: 979-8-88775-765-0 (P)
 ISBN: 979-8-88775-766-7 (E)

Because of the dynamic nature of the Internet, any web addresses or links contained in this book may have changed since publication and may no longer be valid.

The views expressed in this work are solely those of the author and do not necessarily reflect the views of the publisher, and the publisher hereby disclaims any responsibility for them.

CONTENTS

Introduction 1

The Active Journey 3

Grandparenting Tips 4

Loosening The Reigns, Letting Go 8

Enjoying Calm And Managing Turbulence 9

A Discussion With Grandchildren On Maintaining Communal Connectedness 11

Internalizing Positive Attitudes And Qualities About The "Self"
    Part 1: "Self-Image" And "Self-Direction" 14

Strengthen Positives Attitudes And Actions Of The "Self"
    Part 2: Positive "Self-Esteem" And Positive "Self-Dimension" 17

Strengthening Positive Attitudes And Qualities About The "Self"
    Part 3: Positive "Self-Expectancy" And Positive "Self-Motivation" .. 20

Strengthening Positive Attitudes And Qualities About The "Self"
    Part 4: Positive "Self-Control" And Positive "Self-Discipline" . 23

Generation Z Teens 27
    Sharing And Learning 28
    Assisting Them To Learn, Apply And Maintain 32

Informed Generation Z Teens:
    Organize Your Time, Own Your Effects 36

Tips For Generation Z Grandchildren
    Planning, Moving, Doing, Changing 46

References 48

INTRODUCTION

As I was attempting to share my experience on the journey with grandchildren, I became aware that this could be two documents—one for grandparents and one for Generation Z grandchildren. However, in my quest to keep them—grandparents and grandchildren—close, I tried to maintain one document about a family with two parts (first and third) in which the parents are absent. In keeping with this family chronology, grandparents first and grandchildren second, I am continuing the "Journey."

****

When grandparents take on the job and the mission of providing fulltime care for grandchildren, they begin a familiarly unfamiliar journey which requires relearning and continual learning to travel the active, family journey.

Grandparents' ambivalence about their abilities, and indeed, strength and energy as well as grandchildren's well-being can be a little stressful. However, because of the unwavering love and dedication to fostering grandchildren's growth and development, we give ourselves considerable self-talk, collaborate with other resources and alter the map as needed to continue the journey.

While grandparenting is not performed in outlined, sequential order, we must keep in mind that **order** is essential for raising grandchildren; a different, sometimes difficult task when competing with outside influences such as peer pressure, social media, and technology, to name a few.

We must teach and encourage grandchildren to continue to live the Life Skills (Kovalik) learned in elementary school, which will enhance family connectedness for **affective** and **effective** life-long learning as well as promote personal, social, academic, and economic growth and development.

We must also introduce and encourage grandchildren to learn and practice the attitudinal and action qualities of the "*Self*"—image and -direction; -esteem and -dimension; -expectancy and -motivation; -control and -discipline.

THE ACTIVE JOURNEY

A Fulltime Endeavor Which Embody the Following Characteristics:

Love - nurturing, guiding, sharing, supporting

Work - the mission, ***responsibility***; the job, ***role; function***

Ambivalence - inconsistency, psychological stress, self-contradiction

Calm - moderation, tranquility, serenity

Wondering - amazement, surprise, admiration, fascination

Turbulence - agitation, disorder, rebellion

Questioning - curiosity, doubtfulness, uncertainty

Pleasure - enjoyment, amusement, pleasantness

Appreciation - acknowledgement, respectfulness, gratitude

Excitement - interest, emotion, sensitize

Success - accomplishment, victory, prosperity

GRANDPARENTING TIPS

When grandparents suddenly find themselves in the trenches of raising/supporting their *Generation Z grandchildren*, it can be, and often is, a life-changing experience. Depending on the grandchildren's age, grade level, energy and world views, grandparents might need to consult several resources prior to embarking on the "Journey."

If you become grandparent caregivers of infants, you will need to transform your home to almost *all-things-baby*, (or at least to almost *all-things-young*). There are many things babies must have (you will give them more), and there are things you want them to have; you will give those, too, and more. Remember the things you did with your children during their developmental years.

Depending on the time you begin and the duration of the "Journey," you will prepare for and grandparent from one to five stages—infancy/early childhood, pre- school, elementary school, middle school, and high school (maybe college).

Depending on your age, health and outlook, this can seem like a lifetime. Each stage includes unique and specific duties (for those who have forgotten or never knew), beginning with

Infancy. Frequent feedings/formula—organic vs. Traditional, diapering, bathing, clothing, sleeping (duration before waking for feeding/changing every two to four hours a night). Babies must have proper furniture and bedding. They require and grandparents must make scheduled medical visits to stay abreast of baby's physical growth and development. As months pass, you will assist them to focus on various movements to enhance their physical and mental development by talking, reading, and playing with them. You and they will watch and interact with baby TV shows. Grandchildren's healthy development permits them to move from infancy to

Preschool. This milestone can be *traumatic* for both grandparents and grandchildren, which can last for shorter or longer periods. As the little ones are accepted, welcomed, and nurtured by their new teacher, they begin to adjust to being away from their grandparent(s) a few hours a day. Their personal and social development include daily interactions with classmates and friends, going on field trips, attending birthday parties and playdates. They grow socially, intellectually, and kinesthetically—sharing, reading, writing, computing, problem solving, using technology, and participating in group activities which get them ready for

Elementary School. At this level, grandchildren become more independent thinkers and doers, and feel comfortable making friends and engaging in larger group activities. As they grow and move into and through the grades, their educational activities—skills and abilities—grow and become more defined. General and specific learning disabilities are sometimes recognized and diagnosed at this level in their education. Grandchildren learn and demonstrate character development, which continue to grow as they enter

Middle School. Middle School students are literally and figuratively caught in the middle of K-12 education; they are no longer little children and have not yet become teenagers. They are more physically active; many are academically bright; they experience and demonstrate a broad range of feelings and emotions which require nurturing, supporting, patience, understanding and trusting. This is a point in their lives when mood disorders become more apparent—outbursts, stresses, tensions, sadness, etc. They also learn to cope with distractions and focus on personal issues with the help of grandparents, educators, and support personnel. As grandparents, we remain focused with unconditional love and support, as grandchildren's personal identities come into focus and become more defined as they move through the middle grades and enter

High School. Many students at the high school level are more self-directed, self-motivated, and self-controlled in their academic preparation and personal-social behavior. They realize that their academic studies must be geared toward ***general*** and ***specific*** knowledge, as well as college and career preparation. We assist them to become self-advocates—realizing and following through when they need to seek guidance and follow-up with teachers, counselors, and mentors regarding college information—applications, course requirements, standardized tests, and entrance exams.

Generation Z, being *"now"* people, are continually challenging, moving, and changing in their quest for immediate gratification. We are charged with assisting, supporting, encouraging and being catalysts in the pursuit of their gratifications.

LOOSENING THE REIGNS, LETTING GO

Among the many things Generation Z wants most is to have *free reign—very few, if any, restrictions—*allowing them to be, to do and to act (behave) as they wish. Grandparents understand that they cannot always be allowed to demonstrate various behaviors as they wish. They own their feelings, wants and desires; we are charged with their wellbeing, and as such, we must exercise our responsibilities in guiding and encouraging them to behave responsibly and age appropriately. We must assist them to be responsible with emphases on personal, familial, social and task achievements.

While we assist grandchildren in their efforts to move forward in their personal pursuits, which enables them to experience growth and development as individuals, we must be ever mindful of the need to help them observe and be aware of harmful situations as well as practice conventions that promote healthy living and lessen harm *to* themselves and *from* others.

ENJOYING CALM AND MANAGING TURBULENCE

Grandparenting is both a **continuous** and a **continual** *Journey* depending on the health and stamina of the traveler. As with any journey, one is likely to encounter calm (joy) and turbulence (challenge). While our goal of raising grandchildren is to assist them to reach a desired goal, the *journey* of raising grandchildren does not allow one to reach a goal and stop, because the *"goal of life"* is continual and includes continuous **calm** and **turbulence—ups and downs.** We teach them that *we and they are always "becoming," as life is "continual."* We encourage them to be active participants on this journey, thus avoiding complacency and lessening turbulence.

Handling Activities Along the "Journey:" The Job and the Mission.

As grandchildren leave early childhood and move into and through the "tweens and teens," we recognize the behaviors associated with their desire for distance—loosening the reigns, breaking away. Some of these behaviors have distinguishing manifestations—sweet, casual, deliberate, passive and passive aggressive. *Children have an internal GPS (Global Positioning System) that makes them believe that they have all the questions and all the answers to situations in life,* especially when it comes to things they want to do, what they think they should do and what is right for them to do <u>at this moment.</u>

We realize, too, that this is the time to engage them in serious, informed discussions outlining roles and responsibilities of all parties—*grandparents who* **are charged with setting examples—teaching, nurturing, guiding, supporting, sharing,** *and grandchildren who* **are charged with seeking inquisitional information—listening, questioning, learning, following directions, investigating possibilities, and sharing ideas.** Grandparents encourage them to debrief—share concerns, fears, joys, likes and dislikes and ask questions about family, friends, school and the community. We are hopeful that they commit to keeping the "Journey" alive through:

Determination. Vigilance. Hope. Sharing. Faith.

A DISCUSSION WITH GRANDCHILDREN ON MAINTAINING COMMUNAL CONNECTEDNESS

As grandparents, we are charged with supporting our grandchildren's skills and knowledge related to their growth and development and encourage them to **build and maintain communities that embody** the following characteristics:

- Self-respect (pride)
- Respect for others
- Safety
- Health
- Diversity
- Inclusion
- Connectedness

Grandchildren are reminded of their importance to themselves. To carry out their *plans for living and doing commendable things for the community,* they must hold themselves in high regard, thereby demonstrating to the community their

Self-Respect. You appreciate and hold yourself in high esteem. You are mindful of actions and behaviors that demonstrate your presentation to the world. Because of the image of and feeling for yourself, you have

Respect for Others. Expressing concern for the wellbeing of others based on your observed behaviors of their perceived conditions, your offer of assistance and care demonstrate your personal and communal respect. This also includes collaborative effort and commitment to the community and to

Safety. Everyone needs to feel safe in the immediate as well as the surrounding communities. Your awareness of and vigilance for safety help keep people—especially other children, seniors and those who require assistance—out of harm's way. These qualities also assist in promoting and maintaining a community with good mental and physical

Health. Community leaders need to be of sound mind and body if they will be the people to whom others look for guidance. Some of you will be community leaders who will work to cure some of society's problems. As you build communities, you expand your capacity to understand, respect, and accept

Diversity. (Who is invited to the party?) You must embrace human likeness in various cultures--ethnic, race, gender, politics and religion. You must understand that unfamiliar characteristics and behaviors among people that are outside of your experience may not be *wrong* but are simply *different.* Respect and invite

Inclusion. (Offer a place at the table). Inviting, accepting, affirming and respecting positive human characteristics and endeavors give everyone a sense of

Connectedness. Connectedness to whom? What? Connectedness to people, things, and activities that comprise your immediate and surrounding communities. For example—

- Exploring community services
- Sharing the load of home activities—taking care of chores
- Assuming responsibility for younger siblings—reading, playing and sharing
- Serving in the religious community
- Assisting other students at school
- Reaching out to others—making new friends
- Responding to the needs of others—grandparents, senior citizens, neighbors and peers
- Volunteering—Children's Centers, Senior Centers and Non-profit organizations

INTERNALIZING POSITIVE ATTITUDES AND QUALITIES ABOUT THE "SELF"

Part 1: Positive "Self-Image" and Positive "Self-Direction"

Internalizing the positive "Self"—attitudes and qualities—for personal, life-long development is a continuing discussion with grandchildren.

How do grandparents assist grandchildren with the growth and development of positive attitudes (thoughts) and qualities (actions) about the "Self?" These life-long characteristics begin with modeling—being and living the change we want to develop in them. (Remember, much of what they learn from us is **what we do** and some of **what we say**). They remember almost everything that interest them.

Perhaps it is theirs or Mother Nature's way of keeping us honest and alert. Our job is continual-teaching, nurturing, guiding, sharing and supporting; helping them feel good about who they are.

We begin our discussion with the **attitudinal quality** (thinking/feeling) of "self-image" and the **action quality** (doing/producing) of "self-direction." Your "self-image" is your attitude (beliefs, feelings, thoughts) of *who you are and who you want to become.* Your "self-direction" includes the actions you take (your plans, dreams, objectives, activities) *to become who and what you want to be or do.* For example: Your **goal** is to become the person you imagine yourself to be, or to improve the person you are. Your **objective** outlines what you must do to achieve your goal. If your goal is to become an excellent student; an astronaut; a professional actor; a world-class swimmer; a famous model; a professional baseball basketball, football player or golfer; your objective will include these disciplinary activities: education, research, instruction, study, continuous personal practice and observation of outstanding performers in these areas as well as dedicated training and cultivating the positive **attitudinal behavior,** learning and application.

Grandchildren can actualize desired activities by expressing what *they want to do (attitude),* making *attempts to do it (self-direction)* and seeking assistance for proper application. They will be assisted to understand and accept their skills, abilities, limitations and make informed decisions.

Note: let us not forget that we must keep in mind that Generation Zs are basically "Now" persons who want, seek and expect immediate effects, whose goals are measured in hours/days/weeks. Forget the back-in-the-day, "Long-term goals."

Take a character photo. When you look in the mirror and see an image of yourself,

- how do you feel about the person looking back at you?
- what kind of person do you imagine you will become?
- how much time and dedication are you willing to commit to the achievement
- how well do you imagine you will perform?
- how well do you accept failure?
- what do you image you will do in the future?
- do you feel that you will/can win at everything you attempt?
- do you give up easily?
- can you try, try, and try again?
- how many times can you fall, pick yourself up and start again?
- are you willing to take "baby steps" (small attempts) toward you goal?
- who and what will decide how hard you work? You? Circumstances? Peers?

STRENGTHEN POSITIVES ATTITUDES AND ACTIONS OF THE "SELF"

Part 2: Positive "Self-Esteem" and Positive "Self-Dimension"

The Grandparenting Journey includes continuous discussions with grandchildren to assist them to question, examine, seek information about, and to better *understand themselves* thereby enabling them to better understand and be of *service to others.*

The **attitudinal characteristic** of positive "Self-Esteem" is positive feelings of **your** self-worth. The **action quality** of "Self-Esteem"—**positive "Self-Dimension"** —is caring for and supporting the feelings of others (promoting "Other Esteem").

Positive Self-Esteem. We assist grandchildren to think and to speak of themselves in positive terms: "I did a really good job on that report." "My soccer game was over the top." "I realize that the harder I work, the better I perform; I'm getting really good!" "I'm going to help Big Bob improve his game. I hope he will let me." "I'm becoming a really good swimmer. I swim with high school girls/boys and win most of the meets." "I believe in my skills and abilities." "I like how I look."

When grandchildren or anyone change their attitude, they change their performance. ***You compare yourself to yourself.*** As you do good things, concentrate on your successes—skills, abilities, values. You must make changes in your immediate, personal life (your heart, thought processes) rather than looking for external changes. Know that *you* are special and let the world know of your esteem. In your introduction to the world, you will be evaluated on the following characteristics: **how you look; what you say; and most important, <u>what you do.</u>**

Present yourself well. Personal presentation is imbedded in your self-esteem. Try to think before you speak (most of the time). Do the right thing (as often as possible). Most important? Accept and enjoy being **YOU** right now. This might seem to some as being in "overdrive"—beyond self-esteem, but this takes you to the **action quality** of

Positive Self-Dimension. We teach grandchildren to find meaning to life situations beyond ourselves. "Self-Dimension" is reaching beyond yourself. However, you can love and help someone else only to the extent that you can love and respect yourself. Helping others is a great indicator for such a measurement. As with most developmental learning situations, we begin this important task at home with family.

We teach them that their education is life-long—from birth to death—moving, learning, mimicking, making sounds, listening, speaking, reading, sharing, supporting, and observing. We teach them to think and prepare in the **"now"** in their search for the **"tomorrow." Note: Gen Zs are already in the "Now."** The productive **"now"** prepares them for the **healthful, helpful "tomorrow."** By sowing the seeds of **"self"** in grandchildren, we are planting trees under the shade of which others will sit. We **navigate the way** and **enjoy the "Journey."**

We must do and teach them to do "GOOD" for the benefit of ALL.

STRENGTHENING POSITIVE ATTITUDES AND QUALITIES ABOUT THE "SELF"

Part 3: Positive "Self-Expectancy" and Positive "Self-Motivation"

The **attitude** (thinking/feeling) of **"Self-expectancy"** and the **action** (doing/producing) of **"Self-motivation"** are primary characteristics of people who realize and enjoy many successes throughout their lives. We assist our grandchildren to reinternalize and apply these personal characteristics.

Discussions with grandchildren continue as they learn more about themselves. They will learn that they experience success based on their expectations for achievement, thinking continuously about their goals(s), and engaging in activities that produce desired effects (outcomes).

We must teach, assist and support our grandchildren to make and own their successes.

Question: Have you ever wanted to do something so badly that you could hardly wait to get started (a goal)? What did you do first? How often did you think about and/or talk to someone about it? Did you *believe* that you could reach your goal? If so, you were **"self-motivated."**

Everyone is motivated by a feeling, a force or a condition that causes one to act. Motivation may be driven by fear or doubt (perhaps something from the past) or by desire (something in the future), which are two powerful characteristics.

Example: Students who earn high marks (A's/B's) in school generally expect themselves to do so. They often see themselves as high achievers and are disappointed with low marks which they feel do not represent them. They first depend on themselves to get things done, then seek assistance from others as needed to move in the direction of their goal. Think of people you know, or have learned about, who have achieved great thing—personal, societal, communal, historical, educational, political, athletic, entertainment, governmental. How did they make these things happen? _(Exaggeration) These individuals ate, slept and breathed their dreams._

They thought continually about and engaged in an activity(ies) that moved them toward their goal. They were enthusiastic, optimistic and driven. **A strong desire to be, to achieve, and to do something so badly makes you get started.** That strong desire is your motivation, which drives you to act, to do and to produce.

Your affirmation must be: "I expect to achieve my goal; therefore, I will work hard and long to realize my desired effect." Everyone has a reason to perform or not to perform.

Note: Keep in mind that you will need to set aside some "ME TIME" (chill out, do nothing, be-one-with-nature).

How should you react to setbacks, which are inevitable? When something happens to slow progress, carefully examine the circumstances; think of positive changes you can make; generate and discuss ideas with someone you trust to maintain your motivation. Give yourself some "pep-talk" and move toward the finish line.

Enjoy your accomplishments!!!

STRENGTHENING POSITIVE ATTITUDES AND QUALITIES ABOUT THE "SELF"

Part 4: Positive "Self-Control" and Positive "Self-Discipline"

Self-Control (attitude): During our continuous discussion with grandchildren about the "self," we demonstrate and model this personal quality which gives them <u>the leading role in their lives.</u> We teach them by saying, "You realize that **to control means to manage.** In this case, to manage yourself—**how you demonstrate your feelings and your actions.**

When you are in control, you are better able to handle the inevitable ups and downs in your life. Being in control means that you are more likely to behave responsibly, thereby choosing to do what is best for you and others around you. Being in control is taking responsibility for causing your own effects—your own outcomes—in life.

"Self-Control" is a learned behavior. First, let's learn the kinds of real-life feelings you need to control such as anger: frustration, sadness, and embarrassment.

Remember, you are in charge. Learn to make choices. You have the power to make choices about your behavior. <u>No one can take away your power to choose.</u> It is your job to control your feelings (make things happen) instead of your feelings controlling you (letting things happen). Who can manage your feelings better than you?

If you lose control, you cannot put the blame on someone else saying, "That kid, Jo-Jo, made me so mad I had to punch him." You are responsible for what you do about your feelings. Behave properly. When you feel that you have been hurt by someone, use "I" messages to discuss the problem such as, "I feel hurt when you call me names and laugh at me." "I feel sad when you say bad things about me." "I am embarrassed when you tell others that I am dumb and can't read." "I get angry when you try to control the game." Everyone has these feelings from time to time, but controlling them keeps you in charge.

These are tips to help you manage your feelings when they are getting out of control. Recognize these warning signs—racing heartbeat, clenched fists, raising your voice. Stay away, as much as possible, from people or things that upset you. Believe that you have the power (mental ability) to cope with your feelings and solve your problems. Learn to relax and relieve the stress. Take a few deep breaths, relax, do some self-talk (the "Self" is one of your best friends); exercise; talk to someone (a parent, another adult, a friend) about your feelings. You can also **tackle the problem, not the person.** Put yourself in the other person's position. Consider his or her point of view.

Self-Discipline (Action). This quality is *doing **What** has to be done **When** it has to be done.* **Self-discipline is doing within—continually working on** <u>*changing the mental self*</u> **in order to continue** <u>*developing the physical self.*</u> Diligent and persistent hard work is the pain you endure for getting things done and enjoying success. Whether you are working to change feelings or actions, the operations are: practice, practice, practice in order to realize success.

Developing self-discipline requires persistent thinking about your What? When? How? Why? You cannot work on your discipline only once a week. That's far too little time. As you know, being an outstanding baseball player, a world-class swimmer, a skillful skater, an Olympic skier or musician requires organized practice, and continual visualization—seeing yourself winning and/or having won and looking forward to the next game or competition.

Nothing in your behavior maters without self-discipline (if you are mentally and physically able). Self-discipline must be practiced at home, at school, at church and in the larger community. Try to be disciplined everywhere, all the time. This is not an easy, carefree activity. You must be able to

    Listen.
        Observe.
            Practice.
                Learn.
                    Apply.

You never stop learning in the maintenance of your "Self-Discipline" and your "Self-Control."

GENERATION Z TEENS

The Journey into and through **"Teenage"** requires various navigational changes such as:

    Active listening
    Following directions
    Expressing feelings
    Demonstrating responsibility
    Developing and applying ***attitudinal*** and ***action qualities*** of self-
              image/direction
              esteem/dimension
              expectancy/motivation
              control/discipline

Grandparents teach and teens must learn to
    be consciously aware
    own and celebrate accomplishments
    be cooperative—develop and demonstrate leadership
    make informed decisions
    be honest and trustworthy and, above all,

Believe in themselves and maintain "Hope"

GENERATION Z TEENS:
Sharing and Learning

Sharing the experiences and **supporting the efforts** are inherent in the "Journey."

We want grandchildren to learn and engage in healthy living through our teaching, guiding, supporting and, most importantly, **Modeling—demonstrating the behaviors (albeit imperfect) we want to see in them.** At the same time, we must understand and accept their apparent adolescent pubescent developmental issues.

Points of interest along the "Journey" might include some or all the following whether suggested and/or presented by grandchildren or grandparents:

- family discussions personal talks
- one-on-one sessions
- group meetings
- fun work activities vacations
- physical development (team, individual)
- academic commitment (lifelong learning)
- personal/social assessment and character development

Grandparents assist grandchildren to develop and maintain attitudes and feelings of *"hope" (the belief that what is wanted will happen).* We might ask them to think of something they want to discuss with emphasis on what they can and will do to make it a reality. We continually remind them that being hopeful means being inspired and optimistic about what they want to be, to do, to have and to achieve. A person cannot move if he/she does not remove obstacles, maintain hope, and believe. One cannot rise above one's own limitation. If someone tells you that you cannot do something, you can blow them off and keep on moving, but *if you tell yourself that you cannot, you cannot. You have set your limit!*

Along with being hopeful, grandchildren need to learn, embrace, and actuate the personal-social quality of **leadership.** They must see themselves as leaders. They will not all be leaders of some association, organization, business, group; they can be leaders of themselves with awareness that they will need to seek and heed direction from time to time. They will learn that leadership requires active listening as well as committed participation and cooperation. One positive characteristic of leadership is helping others to perform with persistence, efficiency, and timeliness—making a concerted effort to do *"what"* needs to be done, *"when"* and *"how"* it needs to be done.

We assist grandchildren to take charge of their personal-social and academic development by making **informed decisions.** While we know that they don't have complete control over their lives, they can make age-appropriate decisions on many issues that affect their daily life activities. The term *"informed decisions"* means giving conscious thought before actions to experience positive outcomes and make decisions with useful knowledge. They should be encouraged to refrain from making decisions about matters that affect others—positive or negative—without prior discussion and agreement, regardless of whether they are interacting with friends or family.

Grandchildren must learn and apply ***financial management skills***—savings, spending, and investing money. This process should begin with their allowance or money earned from chores and/or outside work. Most teens need permission to work. If they are old enough to work in an established business, they must have a Work Permit and will be paid by check. ***(Note: State Laws Relating to Minors mandates Student Work Permits be obtained from school and signed by a school official. Students must maintain a certain grade point average for employment).***

How will they handle their earnings? It would be wise to seek advice and assistance from grandparents about whether to open a new or use an existing bank account(s), and

- deposit the total amount in their savings account
- deposit the total amount in their checking account
- deposit a portion in each account
- retain a portion for personal use

Youth Investing Club. A Youth Investing Club is a great, fun, real life financial activity that gives grandchildren the opportunity to learn about money. What is investing club? How does one invest? Why? Learn to buy stocks. What is a stock?

What is long-term investing? What is long-term? Engaging grandchildren in discussions about earning, spending and saving money begins an awareness of financial planning.

We must teach and encourage them to *save, and when possible, invest a portion of all earnings.* Learning to make financial decisions at an early age is essential in planning for their future.

GENERATION Z TEENS:
Assisting Them to Learn, Apply and Maintain

We maintain a healthy relationship with teen/young adult grandchildren. We encourage appropriate discussions about important issues to them. Share, explain and engage them in clearly defined guidelines with emphasis on individual and group behaviors. As with many groups, some things you offer for discussion will not go over well. So, be prepared and don't be too sensitive or upset by expressions such as "Why do I have to listen to this again?"

Give more compliments than criticism. Give positive criticism—inform them of unacceptable behaviors while accepting and enhancing their individual qualities. When criticism is given, **emphasize the inappropriate behavior, not the person.** When disciplining, it is difficult for teenagers to understand the difference between **"behavior vs person."** They feel that their *"being"* is under attack, no separation. Teens tend to internalize and overreact to specific and general issues. ***Help them minimize frustrations and maximize independent thinking and self-motivation. Point out visible and invisible things about them that boost and reinforce pride and individualism.*** Some grandchildren might require more help with organization and planning to enjoy successful outcomes. This might be necessary for children with emotional and learning disabilities. **Ensure them that they are loved with no conditions.**

Expressing Individualism. Character building starts at home. While character development is sometimes school and/or classroom related, grandparents do a great deal of character building during the **"Journey."** Working collaboratively with schools keeps you informed of behaviors (social and academic) and reinforces what you are doing to promote personal-social, academic, spiritual, career and communal development.

Discussion Points for Family Life-Long Learning. Set times for family mental health sessions. Allow individuals to ask clarifying questions, make suggestions, present arguments, discuss personal and family issues, school activities, and friendships or to simply, VENT.

The following might be among some items of discussion for families and teens:

- Demonstrate respect and honesty
  (home, school, and community)
- Assume responsibility for following rules
  (home, school, and community)
- Develop a safe community
  (share and assist)
- Form and maintain friendships
  (be a true friend)
- Be discriminate in your choices in life
  (choose wisely)
- Become life-long learners
  (develop personal-social, and academic skills competencies)
- Ask for help
  (accept guidance from persons you know and trust)
- Be informed
  (read, observe, engage, apply, research, share)
- Listen carefully
  (listening is easy; good listening takes effort. Understand the difference between **_hearing_** and **_listening_**)
- Complete assignments at home and at school
- Understand that making mistakes is part of growth, learning, and development
- Practice healthy living
  (maintain a good diet, exercise regularly)

- Give your best effort
- Financial obligations
  (money: earn, spend, save and invest wisely)
- Understand and accept your limitations; enhance, strengthen and refine your skills and abilities
- Develop and practice moral character
- Decide, record and work on the achievement of attainable goals
- Concentrate on individual competitive, academic excellence
- Plan and complete graduation
  (high school, vocational training, college)
- Plan career choices, changes and employability options

INFORMED GENERATION Z TEENS:
Organize Your Time, Own Your Effects

As you plan your future, consider the following suggestions in relation to time:

TIME TO MAKE DECISIONS	TIME TO WORK	TIME TO "CHILL OUT"

Let's talk to one another about **"Organizing Your Time."** For this discussion, to **"Organize Your Time"** is to **"Manage Your Time."** Can you really manage time? <u>**Can you manage yourself in a given amount of time?**</u> Time is value; it has many meanings and can be assessed according to its usefulness in performance.

Note: in employment, "Time" is usually referred to as "Money"—Time is money! For example, you have a job that requires you to produce 12 items in an hour to defend its production cost and sale price. You produce only 6 items. How long will you be able to perform at this rate before losing your job? Use your time wisely!

Do **what** <u>has to be done</u> **when** it <u>has to be done.</u>

If you can find a way to accomplish a task (homework, chores, job duties,) *with minimum effort, maximum efficiency and make the fewest wrong turns, you have learned to* <u>organize</u> *and work* <u>efficiently</u> (producing a desired outcome with minimum effort) within a specified period time. This process is referred to as *working, studying smarter, not harder.* This work ethic applies to grandparents as well. Make this a habit; learn and benefit from it for a lifetime.

If you have homework assignments to do and want to participate in some social activity you really like, you will be able to do both because efficient management of homework gives you more free time. You see, efficiency allows you to spend less time on homework and learn more in the process.

The **Key** is **Organization.** How organized are you? If you are a person who keeps things in order, you are ahead of many others. But, if you are among those who never know where the entire binder is—part in the locker; part at home; some on the school yard; some left on the bus; and part in the washing machine—Boy!, you need help!! This really happens. Bits and pieces of paper, books and notebooks have been turned in to me at school from a city bus driver, from the laundromat and from the sandwich shop. Do you know anyone (from the lack of organization) who brings the wrong books to class, has no pen or pencil, and studied the wrong assignment? **This person needs help, badly. Let us offer our help!!**

The first step in organizing your time is to decide

HOW you expect to achieve your goals given the realities of time-wasting that we all experience from time to time. When you get activities in sync with your overall plans, determine

WHY you are doing certain things and not others. Clearly decide

WHAT you want to achieve and the amount of time you are willing to invest

A busy person needs a guide or a map to keep up with activities. Such a guide might be a weekly calendar to record things that need to be done. You might ask, why do we need to record everything to be done? By recording all planned activities, you can determine the amount of time needed for certain tasks. For long-term activities—projects, reports, examinations, etc.—you can utilize the helpfulness of your computer, or the calendar app on your phone. If you do not have a computer, purchase some poster sheets to plan study activities by drawing horizontal and vertical lines to form blocks for dates, descriptions, materials and supplies. **Hand in assignments on time.**

Place the chart in your room near your study area. Make sure it is visible, so that your activities will always be within you reach. There is no sense making a chart or recording information if you do not check it.

You will become **a more interesting person** and will be more **interested** in preparing assignments. You will study more efficiently; your grades will improve significantly! You will be happy! And, the thermostat of your "self-esteem" (self-worth—holding yourself in high regard; positive feelings about yourself) will reach a high point on your **internal thermometer of "self-satisfaction."**

Do you really want to improve yourself, assist your classmates, your parents, anyone? Say, "Yes!" Once you learn to do something well (the way it should be done) you can **adapt** (change) and **adopt** (take on) other things to suit your needs. Since you always want to be organized, (your life will be so much more peaceful, and you will wonder if it is really you) use the **Calendar, Project Board, or Computer effectively.** Work with a "Winning attitude" because

Winners MAKE things happen
Losers LET things happen
YOU ARE A WINNER!!

Once you learn which study habits and patterns work for you, **hone** (sharpen—practice, own) them, but be flexible and add new techniques learned from other sources. Also, be flexible and drop activities/techniques that are no longer useful. Most importantly, set the rules and stick to them as closely as possible keeping in mind that you should

PLAN AHEAD.

> *"The day on which one starts out, is not the time to start one's preparation."*
> African Proverb-Nigeria

Know what you must do and plan to take care to get it done. Get accurate information from those who would give assignments. If you do not understand what is expected, you will be anxious and waste time doing unnecessary, inaccurate work. You will hand it in to the teacher; it will not be accepted; or, if it is you will receive a poor grade because it is incorrect or is not what was assigned. You get upset and say, "Well you didn't explain it, and I didn't know it." **Get directions before starting your work!** *You must ask for clarification. Advocate for yourself.* So, Ask. Ask. Ask. Ask until you receive understandable, satisfactory answers. Teachers want you to ask questions for clarification and understanding; they realize that you are interested and want to do well. Think Win! Win! Proceed with the assignment. That way, you will do it correctly the first time.

If your assignment or project is due April 1, and you complete it on March 29, how would you feel? Remember, when you plan, you have time for other things—movies, games, leisure. Keep in mind that when you **"fail to plan,"** **you "plan to fail."**

STAY CURRENT. Keep your Calendar, Project Board and Computer up to date. Never forget to make notations of things important to—

- assignments
- appointments
- notes (for each class)
- books/supplies (purchase or return)
- Make your equipment and supplies your friend; they will not let you down.

We have discussed quite a bit about ORGANIZING YOUR TIME. It has been repeated much. That's okay. *Repetition is a good skill-builder.* Ask any professional performer, athlete, dancer, singer, or speaker about it. For study and achievement, find a balance, a comfortable point and avoid cramming or wasting time because in learning for and about yourself, you must

BE REALISTIC. Take care to lessen the stress. You know the type of person you are—your skills, abilities, aptitude, etc., so **plan your schedule and goals, not someone else's.** You can neither plan for, learn for, nor be anyone else. You can be only YOU. You can assist someone else; take care of yourself, first. Listen to and accept assistance and guidance from trusted sources, but keep in mind the importance of your own uniqueness, because

> *"You are the only person who can use your ability.
> It is an awesome responsibility."*
>
> Zigler

There might be times when you are trying to stay on top of your work, but things start running together causing confusion and headaches. These situations probably mean that you are attempting to do too many things at one time.

Decide which job, task, or assignment to complete first. Lessen the stress and you will be more productive. To avoid anxiety-producing situations

SET PRIORITIES. Be honest about assignments which require more time and effort—those which you dislike most and those on which you perform less well. *By the way,* ***always take some time for yourself to just be with YOU, doing nothing.***

If you are not functioning well, no amount of planning, setting priorities or anything else will make a difference, you will be unproductive. To prioritize is to list tasks and determine how much time to devote to each. Plan fun, easy activities ***after*** critical study time so that they will be incentives, not distractions. Keep in mind the need to

BE FLEXIBLE. You can plan carefully and comprehensively. You think you are set. Everything is in place. Go! You receive another assignment. Your Calendar is fully planned—every hour filled. What do you do? ***Start Over!*** Adjust your plans. Seek help to solve your dilemma. The assignment has to be completed. You cannot ignore it. You might have to change the whole day's plan. Be flexible and be ready to

MONITOR AND ADJUST. Monitor your progress at various periods; adjust where necessary. Only you know how you intended for your study schedule to work. You will need to adjust if you have allotted too much or too little time to one assignment. ***Flexibility is crucial.*** Suppose you get a cold, become ill, and fall behind. You might even stay healthy and get ahead. Enjoy some quiet time. Take time to relax, reflect, exercise, talk to a classmate, a friend or just do nothing. ***Take time for yourself.***

Make your Calendar, Project Board or Power Point attractive and stand out by prioritizing tasks in color. For example,

RED - must be accomplished this week
BLUE - to be completed in two weeks
YELLOW- for personal time (appointments, dates)
GREEN - for classes and evaluations

You can briefly see what to do and when to do it. Keep in mind that you need to concentrate on

ONE THING AT A TIME. Accomplish one thing effectively and efficiently before moving to something else. Moving from one thing to another and completing nothing is confusing and time wasting. Complete one task, then go to the next. Do one organized thing at a time and

STAY ON TRACK. Be self-directed. "Do not respond to the urgent and forget the important." (Fry). You are studying. You receive a phone call or a text message.

You have been waiting to hear from someone special. Do you throw away the pen/pencil/book, respond to the call or text and engage in long conversation? You were studying. Can the call or text wait for you to jot down a note indicating where you stopped? Can you answer quickly informing the person that you must complete an assignment and will talk later?

Distractions will take you off track, break your concentration, and consume precious time. Try not to permit too many distractions. Sometimes you must say "No." You will have to skip your favorite TV show many times unless you are ahead on your Calendar, Project Board, or Power Point assignments. Staying on track avoids starting over. However, sometimes you must start over (when you believe that you have done everything right) because you forgot something. And, Oh Yes!

AVOID UNINVITED GUESTS. Inform your friends, acquaintances, classmates, pets, and relatives of your new goal. Hold firmly to the schedule you set. Try not to be too concerned about the negative comments you are bound to receive.

Stay on track. Your tenacious desire to succeed and your get-things-done attitude will make a difference in your life and might rub off on others.

REMEMBER, YOU CANNOT <u>BE</u> EVERYTHING.
YOU CANNOT <u>DO</u> EVERYTHING.

BUT YOU CAN <u>BE ORGANIZED</u> —EFFICIENT, EFFECTIVE, ON-TIME AND PRODUCTIVE.

Tips for Generation Z Grandchildren
Planning, Moving, Doing, Changing

You are Generation Z! You are inquisitive, educated, independent thinkers, persistent, involved, decisive, competitive, leaders, trend-setters, and much more.

You cannot permit yourselves to be bored. So, challenge yourselves to do the following **life things** and live your lives to the fullest, knowing that there is

- A dream to follow
- A goal to set
- A plan to make
- A project to begin
- An idea to put into action
- A possibility to explore
- An opportunity to grasp
- A choice to make
- A mystery to unfold
- A journey to take
- A pain to endure
- A prayer to answer

In your quest to keep it simple, beautiful, and rewarding, know that life is

- A mystery: Research it
- A journey: Travel it
- Painful: Endure it
- Beautiful: Observe it
- Funny: Laugh at it

- A song: Sing it
- A flower: Smell it
- Wonderful: Enjoy it
- A candle: Light it
- Precious: Behold it
- A gift: Open it
- Love: Give it
- Light: Shine in it

Be Vigilant!   **Be Happy!**   **Be Strong!**   **Choose Wisely!**   **Live Well!**

REFERENCES

Davis, M. E. *Standards-Based Counseling in the Middle School.* Bloomington, IN: First Books. 2002.

Davis, M. E. *The Grandparenting Journey: Leading the Way.* Bloomington, IN: AuthorHouse. 2010.

Karlitz, Gail and Honig, Debbie. *Growing Money: A Complete Investing Guide for Kids.* PSSI-Price Stern Sloan. An Imprint of Pinguin Group (USA) Inc. 2010.

Waitley, Dennis E. *The Psychology of Winning.* (Audio Tapes).

www.ingramcontent.com/pod-product-compliance
Lightning Source LLC
LaVergne TN
LVHW012048070526
838201LV00082B/3853